LATIMER STUDIES 73

PLASTIC PEOPLE

HOW QUEER THEORY IS CHANGING US

BY PETER SANLON

The Latimer Trust

Plastic People: How Queer Theory is Changing Us © Peter Sanlon
2010

ISBN 978-0-946307-83-8

Cover photo © HL – Fotolia.com

Published by the Latimer Trust January 2010

The Latimer Trust (formerly Latimer House, Oxford) is a
conservative Evangelical research organisation within the Church
of England, whose main aim is to promote the history and theology
of Anglicanism as understood by those in the Reformed tradition.
Interested readers are welcome to consult its website for further
details of its many activities.

The Latimer Trust
PO Box 26685, London N14 4XQ UK
Registered Charity: 1084337
Company Number: 4104465
Web: www.latimertrust.org
E-mail: administrator@latimertrust.org

Views expressed in works published by The Latimer Trust are those of the
authors and do not necessarily represent the official position of The Latimer
Trust.

CONTENTS

1.   Plastic People

Jesus said, "Every female who makes herself male will enter the kingdom of Heaven."

The Gospel of Thomas.

It is doubtful that the arguments for and against homosexual practice in the Christian church can be stated with any greater clarity or prolixity than they have been in the past few years. We are not adding words to that debate. The issue that concerns us is not homosexuality *per se* but rather the conditions of belief in our culture.

Technological and medical discoveries are enabling humanity to remould bodies and change genders, with a degree of success previously unimaginable. One researcher observed:

> We take it for granted that we maintain the sex we are born with, including whether we have testes or ovaries. But this work shows that the activity of a single gene, FOXL2, is all that prevents adult ovary cells turning into cells found in testes.[1]

While such medical advances are being made, it is important for Christians to realise that the conceptual self-understandings of secular persons, provide the cultural context for how these developments are understood, used, celebrated, pursued or rejected. Too often society assumes that if something is possible, it is good. Far too frequently such an implicit argument is portrayed as value free. Unless the church exposes the cultural assumptions and intellectual

---

[1] Robin Lovell-Badge, quoted in The Times, Dec. 11, http://www.timesonline.co.uk/tol/news/science/genetics/article6952050.ece

conceptions which frame and underlie such dogmas, we will remain ineffective at communicating the Gospel. Examining some of the dogmatic assumptions of secular approaches to the nature of humanity, is one of the main aims of this study. It is embarked upon with the hope of clearing the way for more meaningful preaching, outreach and pastoral care.

Acceptance and celebration of homosexuality (and a number of related aspects of gender and sexuality) are creedal in secularity. While there have been countless popular-level accounts of cultural aspects of this development – the 1960's, contraception, feminism, urbanisation, media etc. – less has been said about the philosophic-theological writings which underpin the gay/lesbian movement. The scholarly writings of the gay/lesbian academic guild are not readily accessible as they often utilise a style which is dense and self-referential. They build upon specific schools of Continental Philosophy,[2] Freudian psychoanalysis and post-structuralism. Obscure art-house films and treatises from Plato, Derrida and Foucault are discussed in a manner which assumes the reader is familiar with their details. Biographical ruminations blend with political and philosophical observations. Doubtless the writings we are referring to here have not had a wide readership – yet they are not only the backbone of the modern gay/lesbian movement, they have successfully changed the way heterosexual people, young and old, view themselves and the world:

> What I call 'the gay thing' is something which has just happened, and is happening, to all of us, whatever our own sexual orientation is. You can be as straight as you like, but being straight is no longer the same as it was when there was no such thing as 'gay.' Our picture of what it is to be male or female has undergone, and is undergoing, huge changes which affect us not only from without, but from within. We find ourselves relating, whether we want to or not, with each

---

[2] An excellent introduction is David West, *An Introduction to Continental Philosophy* (Cambridge: Polity Press, 1996).

other, and with ourselves, in new ways as a result of something which is far bigger than any of us.[3]

Until recently people thought of themselves as single or married. Now it is difficult to not be conscious of being a *straight* single, or a *gay* person in a civil partnership. Public debate about gay 'marriage' has a real impact on how *both* straight and gay people view themselves; as do television programmes about gender reallocation operations, pop songs about lesbianism and so forth. We have all become in meaningful ways, plastic people.

Queer writers are aware of these developments and have been instrumental in bringing them about. They realise that using terms such as 'Queer' has changed all people:

> When the term has been used as a paralyzing slur, as the mundane interpolation of pathologized sexuality, it has produced the user of the term as the emblem and vehicle of normalization; the occasion of its utterance, as the discursive regulation of the boundaries of sexual legitimacy. Much of the straight world has always needed the queers it has sought to repudiate through the performative force of the term.[4]

Christians ought to cultivate empathic understanding of the concerns and methods of these writers – self-designated as 'Queer' lesbian/gay thinkers. For as all people in our culture have been impacted by the queer movement, the conditions of belief have been altered. Central aspects of Christianity simply do not make sense to a generation that has been 'queered.' If we want to evangelise our generation, we must understand it. We need to realise how it has come to be that the sacrament of homosexuality signifies more than bread and wine.

Attempting sympathetically to understand Queer writers is one small, but essential part, of appreciating what Charles Taylor has

---

[3] James Alison, "The Gay Thing: Following the Still Small Voice," in *Queer Theology: Rethinking the Western Body*, ed. Gerard Loughlin (Oxford: Blackwell, 2007). p.51.

[4] Judith Butler, *Bodies That Matter: On the Discursive Limits of Sex* (London: Routledge, 1993). p.223.

described:

> The shift to secularity consists of a move from a society where belief in God is unchallenged and indeed, unproblematic, to one in which it is understood to be one option among others, and frequently not the easiest to embrace.[5]

Queer thinking has impacted our entire culture. On both sides of the gay/lesbian debates, inside and outside the church, we have all been changed. Our denials, affirmations, identities, concerns and agendas – we have all become plastic people who can be remoulded.

One of the failings of Christian engagement with cultural and academic phenomena has been our tendency to generalise and be reductionistic. An important example of this which is pertinent to our topic, is the attitude to 'postmodernity' in evangelical writings and church life. Many have written against postmodernity, warning of its dangers and excesses. Others have seen words or ideas in postmodernity which may be embraced as conducive to evangelism or church life. Both rejection and acceptance is reductionistic, for postmodernity is a diffuse variegated cultural phenomenon. Some aspects of it are good and others bad. What Peter Berger wrote of modernity applies to postmodernity also: it 'is a relative phenomenon; it is one moment in the historical movements of human consciousness – not its pinnacle, or its culmination, or its end.'[6] Some of the good aspects could be used in unhelpful ways. Some of the bad could be rejected in unhelpful ways. At stake are not just facts and histories, but attitudes and postures. Bearing this in mind, we will attempt to avoid generalisations, and instead of referring to something like 'postmodernity' will engage with specific writers. We will quote them extensively, as they are not widely known outside their guild. This will give a sense of the style of the writings (for the style is part of the power) and will hopefully enable us to understand

---

[5] Charles Taylor, *A Secular Age* (Cambridge: Belknap Press, 2007). p.3.
[6] Peter Berger, *The Heretical Imperative: Contemporary Possibilities of Religious Affirmation* (London: Collins, 1980). p.10.

the concerns of at least a representative sample of queer thinkers. Before we proceed to that, and subsequent implications for practical ministry, it will be helpful to consider the history of gay/lesbian academic study.

2.   History of Gay/Lesbian Studies

Gay/Lesbian writers are extremely conscious of the history of their movement; the social settings of the various stages of past development and future aspirations. The narrative of their history is told, not only with the aim of furthering their goals, but also as part of a project of relativisation:

> Sex has no history. It is a natural fact, grounded in the functioning of the body, and as such, it lies outside of history and culture... Unlike sex, sexuality is a cultural production... Sexuality then, does have a history.[7]

The 'cultural production' of sexuality and the relativististic consequences of this (partially true) insight, will become an important part of our analysis. The move from historical diversity to moral relativity is so well-worn now that it is assumed without defence in recent textbooks:

> That certain conventional ways of doing gender are natural can be challenged by looking at the different ways that gender has been done throughout history... This all indicates that gender is something that we learn to do.[8]

In the 1960s and '70s gay/lesbian studies were mainly sociological studies on sexual behaviour regarded as unusual or deviant. This was initially indebted to Freud,[9] and then gathered pace as a result of the

---

[7] David M. Halperin, "Is There a History of Sexuality?," in *The Lesbian and Gay Studies Reader*, ed. Abelove, Barale, and Halperin (London: Routledge, 1993). p.416.

[8] Mary Holmes, *Gender and Everyday Life* (London: Routledge, 2009). p.56.

[9] For Freud, the unusual or deviant was studied as a means of understanding normal psychology. Some Queer writers today maintain in that vein that the best way to understand heterosexuality, is to study homosexuality. The language of deviancy was that used by Freud and was not a moral evaluation.

development of sociological research generally. As a body of literature developed, the focus became not merely the behaviours themselves, but the reaction to them of society.[10]

The outbreak of the AIDS virus in the 1980s hijacked the trajectory of gay/lesbian studies. Interest turned almost exclusively to the medical causes of AIDS, and the media response to the illness. AIDS kick-started a strand of gay/lesbian writing which continues to the present; exploring the implications of AIDS for gay/lesbian identity.[11] While sociological studies were almost exclusively dominated by AIDS, the English translation of Foucault's work *The History of Sexuality Vol.1* both challenged received views of the history of sexuality and marked a new focus on theoretical linguistic research.

Foucault's book (which is surprisingly lucid, short and witty) is an astonishing tour de force. Reading it is still one of the best ways to appreciate something of what drives and shapes the scholars now known as Queer. Foucault knew he was a revolutionary. So he wrote that when speaking about sex:

> We are conscious of defying established power, our tone of voice shows that we know we are being subversive, and we ardently conjure away the present and appeal to the future, whose day will be hastened by the contribution we believe we are making. Something that smacks of revolt, of promised freedom... slips easily into this discourse on sexual oppression.[12]

In contrast to the simplistic popular historical narrative of Victorian repression which built upon Christian morals, Foucault argued that

---

[10] Ken Plummer, "Mapping the Sociological Gay: Past, Presents and Futures of a Sociology of Same Sex Relations," in *Lesbian and Gay Studies*, ed. Theo Sandfort, et al. (London: Sage Publications, 2000). p.49.

[11] Lee Edelman, *Homographesis: Essays in Gay Literary and Cultural Theory* (London: Routledge, 1994). p.79-117.

[12] Michel Foucault, *The Will to Knowledge*, vol. 1, *The History of Sexuality* (London: Allen Lane, 1979). p.6-7.

the way society had talked about sex, created complex, variegated power structures which actually inform and shape our sexuality:

> We are dealing not nearly so much with a negative mechanism of exclusion as with the operation of a subtle network of discourses, special knowledges, pleasures and powers.[13]

Deconstructing and exposing the nature of these discourses of power was to become the main focus of what became Queer studies. Foucault's writings shifted the academic focus from sociological matters to do with AIDS, to theoretical investigations of language and power.[14]

On the back of Foucault, gay/lesbian academics turned to theoretical issues of language – with a very real focus upon politics, law and culture. The actual word 'Queer' represents much of what the project was about. Queer was originally an insult thrown at gays, but from the Stonewall Riot onwards:

> Lesbians and gay men celebrate their increased public presence, as well as the effrontery, subversion, and difference of queer style and politics. They now challenge homophobia by chanting 'We're queer, we're here, get used to it.'[15]

Reclaiming the word Queer (as the church did with 'Christian') was emblematic of the subversive victory Queer theorists would win against considerable odds. It conveys the idea of changing the current order, subverting expectations and giving voice to the marginalised:

> To 'queer' things means to mess them up, to pull apart the straightness of the social world and encourage more playful and diverse ways of living pleasurable lives.[16]

---

[13] Ibid. p.72.

[14] Plummer, "Mapping the Sociological Gay: Past, Presents and Futures of a Sociology of Same Sex Relations." p.51.

[15] Bryne Fone, *Homophobia* (New York: Metropolitan Books, 2000). p.411.

[16] Holmes, *Gender and Everyday Life*. p.121.

Queer theorists aimed to bring to the surface the assumptions latent in culture, which denied a just treatment of gays. For example, considerable writing was done about the 1992 Hollywood film *Basic Instinct*, in which Sharon Stone played a beautiful lesbian homicidal manic, who murdered heterosexual men during intercourse. Some Queer theorists appreciated the movie as they saw any mainstream portrayal of lesbians as helpful. Others traced the origins of the character played by Stone back to the literary figures of threatening lesbian vampires – such as those in Bram Stoker's *Dracula*.[17] Considered in such a light, *Basic Instinct* was yet another attempt by heterosexuals to stereotype lesbians in order to exert power over them.[18]

As may be realised from this example, Queer writing engaged with films, music, novels and photography – as well as ancient and modern philosophy. The nature of 'gay films' were pondered – could those which portrayed stereotypes and demonised gays be reclaimed?[19] Hidden meanings and the assumptions in words were played with, in an attempt to expose aspects of discourse which needed to be challenged. The literature which evolved exalted sex, gender and sexuality to a central place in society. Unsurprisingly, parallels were drawn with feminism:

> Women's history seeks to establish the centrality of gender as a fundamental category of historical analysis and understanding ... Thus women's studies is not limited to the study of women's lives and contributions: it includes any research that treats gender as a central category of analysis... Lesbian/gay studies does for sex and sexuality approximately

---

[17] Bram Stoker, *Dracula* (Ware: Wordsworth Classics, 1993). p.33.

[18] Marco Pustianaz, "Fashionably Queer: Lesbian and Gay Cultural Studies," in *Lesbian and Gay Studies*, ed. Theo Sandfort, et al. (London: Sage Publications, 2000). p.169–70.

[19] Marco Pustianaz, "Gay Male Literary Studies," in *Lesbian and Gay Studies*, ed. Theo Sandfort, et al. (London: Sage Publications, 2000). p.149.

what women's studies does for gender.[20]

Foucault, of course, would say that such a project only exposes the true reality of what has been latent in culture all along – 'Sex, the explanation for everything.'[21] As this project gathered pace, the word 'Queer' transcended its limits as a noun, to function as a verb. Academics began 'to queer' other disciplines. Law, philosophy, history, science and economics – all could be deconstructed and seen through the new lens of Queer thinking. The jewel in the crown is, naturally – Queering the queen of sciences: Theology.[22] The sheer breadth and complexity of work undertaken in 'Queering' other disciplines is breathtaking:

> None of these domains – politics, desire, gender, sexuality, representation – is primary, determining all the rest. Their very unpredictability creates the fascination, and the importance of these topics for queer theorists. But it is clear, at least to queer theorists, that we cannot fully understand any of these domains except as we understand how they interact.[23]

This brings us to the current reality of Queer Theory. It is a hugely ambitious academic project which seeks to re-imagine all aspects of human existence. The inter-connectedness of all subject matters causes readers to doubt that they can ever really reach final answers. Questions are open-ended. There is always another, more subversive, more Queer, way of looking at what you once took for granted. In a generation which ignores the great philosophical traditions of the past, Queer writers assume a detailed knowledge of them and then revise in exciting ways. While many academics retreat from society, Queer theorists are ever conscious of the implications of their work

---

[20] Abelove, Barale, and Halperin, eds., *The Lesbian and Gay Studies Reader* (London: Routledge, 1993). p.xv.

[21] Foucault, *The Will to Knowledge*. p.78.

[22] Gerard Loughlin, ed., *Queer Theology: Rethinking the Western Body* (Oxford: Blackwell, 2007).

[23] William B. Turner, *A Genealogy of Queer Theory* (Philadelphia: Temple University Press, 2000). p.4.

for real life:

> Lesbian/gay studies has an oppositional design. It is informed by the social struggle for sexual liberation, the personal freedom, dignity, equality and human rights of lesbians, bisexuals and gay men; it is also informed by resistance to homophobia and heterosexism ... Lesbian/gay studies necessarily straddles scholarship and politics.[24]

Queer academic writing often contains observations which appear at first to be illogical, jejune or fanciful. It would be a grave mistake to dismiss this body of work in such a manner. The very point of Queer writing is to subvert and change the way we look at life. It is intimately connected to post-structuralist Continental Philosophy, which is itself a reaction against the rationalism of the Enlightenment. Throwing at Queer writers accusations of being illogical or wrong, simply results in the accuser being dismissed as modernist and rationalistic. There is often a wry, knowing smile in Queer writing, which echoes that of Derrida and Foucault. It is very difficult to know how seriously to take individual claims; a comment may be made to provoke a reaction or expose an assumption, more than as an empirical fact. When all of reality is contingent upon discourse, words are used as means of power rather than bearers of truth. This is as much the case when the speaker is the repressed minority seeking to subvert, as when one is the monolithic authoritative ruler. In any case, Queer academics merit being sympathetically considered on their own terms, because their project has enjoyed phenomenal success in the modern world and church.

One example of this practical success may be seen in modern curriculums of schools. When the British government was considering repealing Article 28, which outlawed promoting homosexuality in schools, the language used at the time, with concomitant assumptions, was carefully analysed and deconstructed by Queer theorists:

---

[24] Abelove, Barale, and Halperin, eds., *The Lesbian and Gay Studies Reader.* p.xvi.

Behind the rhetoric that identifies the supposedly widespread and perilous 'promotion' of homosexuality lies a particularly dense core of fantasy and denial that needs to be carefully unpacked if the rhetoric is to be successfully countered.[25]

Watney articulated that the law could only be changed if people's inner attitudes and assumptions were remoulded. Back in 1982, another Queer writer reflected on the progress that had been, and needed to be made, in altering attitudes via school curriculums:

How can deeply entrenched attitudes and behaviour be confronted and changed? Certainly gay and lesbian/feminist activism has made significant inroads since the late 1960s, both in the public sphere and upon the awareness of individuals... They have not had nearly enough impact upon the educational system itself. Curriculum that focuses in a positive way upon issues of sexual identity, sexuality and sexism is still rare, particularly in primary and secondary grades. Yet schools are virtual cauldrons of homophobic sentiment.[26]

The changes made in schooling over the years since the above words were first published are nothing short of breathtaking. Not only are many school teachers unable to share their views openly with children, a worrying number are no longer able to conceive of another way of doing things. The aspirations of Queer theory, as stated in their own words, have been realised to a remarkable degree. We are all plastic people and have been remoulded by the spread of ideas first broached in their writings. This alone means we ought to attempt to understand them on their own terms, avoiding reductionism and seeking to discern their underlying concerns.

---

[25] Simon Watney, "School's Out," in *Inside/Out: Lesbian Theories, Gay Theories*, ed. Diana Fuss (London: Routledge, 1991). p.399.

[26] Barbara Smith, "Homophobia: Why Bring It Up?," in *The Lesbian and Gay Studies Reader*, ed. Abelove, Barale, and Halperin (London: Routledge, 1993). p.101.

3.   Freedom from Gender?

We have already mentioned that Foucault saw himself as a revolutionary seeking liberty in sexual matters. John Coffey has highlighted that Foucault was seeking freedom not just to experience homosexuality and sadomasochism in whatever way he wished (though he was). He was seeking a far more radical freedom:

> In a 1983 interview, Foucault made it clear that he endorsed Nietzsche's views on self-creation. Sartre and California's New Agers had gone awry, he suggested, because they had introduced the notion of 'authenticity', implying that one had to be faithful to one's *true* self. In fact, there was nothing within or without to which one had to be true – self-creation had no such limits. It was about aesthetics, not morals; one's only concern should be to fashion a self that was 'a work of art'.[27]

Freedom has been a key theme in the Queer writing. Epitomised by the image of 'coming out'[28] and building on Foucault's aspirations, Queer writers seek freedom in what may be reasonably construed as radical:

> To destroy 'woman' does not mean that we aim to destroy lesbianism simultaneously with the categories of sex, because lesbianism provides for the moment the only social form in which we can live freely. Lesbian is the only concept I know of which is beyond the categories of sex (woman and man)... For what makes a woman is a specific social relation to a man, a

---

[27] John Coffey, *Life after the Death of God? Michel Foucault and Postmodern Atheism* (1996 [cited 27.8.09]); available from http://www.jubilee-centre.org/document.php?id=15. (Accessed 27.8.09)

[28] Eve Kosofsky Sedgwick, "Epistemology of the Closet," in *The Lesbian and Gay Studies Reader*, ed. Abelove, Barale, and Halperin (London: Routledge, 1993).

relation that we have called servitude, a relation which implies personal and physical obligation as well as economic obligation (forced residence, domestic corvée, conjugal rights, unlimited production of children, etc.), a relation which lesbians escape by refusing to become or stay heterosexual. We are escapees from our class in the same way as American runaway slaves were when escaping slavery and becoming free ... [We seek] the destruction of heterosexuality as a social system which is based on the oppression of women by men and which produces the doctrine of the differences between the sexes to justify this oppression.[29]

Historically, considerable freedom has accrued to homosexuals as a result of economic developments:

Only when individuals began to make their living through wage labour, instead of as parts of an interdependent family unit, was it possible for homosexual desire to coalesce into a personal identity – an identity based on the ability to remain outside the heterosexual family and to construct a personal life based on attraction to one's own sex.[30]

However the freedom being sought by Queer theorists is far more than can ever be achieved by money. Ultimately, Queer theorists seek for a freedom from the limitations of gender itself. Only when humanity understands itself as construed not by biological realities, but malleable sociological relations, will homosexuality be able to be enjoyed without heterosexual oppression. The assumptions latent in a presupposed biological bias towards heterosexuality must be Queered sufficiently that they may be discarded. As can be seen from the above quotations, this vision is held by more than one Queer theorist, and is consistent with the personal aspirations of Michael Foucault. In order to better appreciate the kind of liberty sought by Queer

[29] Monique Wittig, "One Is Not Born a Woman," in *The Lesbian and Gay Studies Reader*, ed. Abelove, Barale, and Halperin (London: Routledge, 1993). p.108.

[30] John D'Emilio, "Capitalism and Gay Identity," in *The Lesbian and Gay Studies Reader*, ed. Abelove, Barale, and Halperin (London: Routledge, 1993). p.470.

academics, we will focus upon the writings of one key thinker – Judith Butler.[31]

Judith Butler was born in 1956 to a French Jewish family. She teaches at the University of California, Berkeley. Butler is one of the world's leading lesbian feminist Queer academics. Her writing is prolific and defies simple categorisation. However a reasonable attempt at a summary is given by Sarah Salih:

> To a greater or lesser extent, all Butler's books ask questions about the formation of identity and subjectivity, tracing the processes by which we become subjects when we assume the sexed/gendered/raced identities which are constructed for us (and to a certain extent by us) within existing power structures.[32]

In the documentary cited above, Butler mentions that from childhood she disliked authority. Much of her academic writing has pursued a form of absolute freedom which she covets for herself:

> The prospect of being anything, even for pay, has always produced in me a certain anxiety, 'to be' gay, 'to be' lesbian seems to be more than a simple injunction to become who or what I already am... I am not at ease with lesbian theories, gay theories, for identity categories tend to be instruments of regulatory regimes.[33]

Her book *Gender Trouble* argued for freedom from gender. Butler's thinking on gender develops from Simone de Beauvoir, who wrote:

> One is not born, but becomes a woman. No biological,

---

[31] An excellent introduction to Judith Butler may be found in an hour long documentary, which includes reflections on her upbringing and scenes of her lectures. Part one of six is available at: http://www.youtube.com/watch?v=Q5onQUGiI3s&feature=related (Accessed 25.08.09)

[32] Sarah Salih, *Judith Butler, Routledge Critical Thinkers* (London: Routledge, 2002). p.2.

[33] Judith Butler, "Imitation and Gender Insubordination," in *Inside/Out: Lesbian Theories, Gay Theories*, ed. Diana Fuss (London: Routledge, 1991). p.13.

psychological, or economic fate determines the figure that the human female presents in society: it is civilization as a whole that produces the creature, intermediate between male and eunuch, which is described as feminine.[34]

Butler cites this famous quotation and extends the idea to suggest that sexed identity itself, is construed by cultural discourse:

> Gender ought not to be construed as a stable identity or locus of agency from which various acts follow; rather, gender is an identity tenuously constituted in time, instituted in an exterior space through a stylized repetition of acts. The effect of gender is produced through the stylization of the body and, hence, must be understood as the mundane way in which bodily gestures, movements, and styles of various kinds constitute the illusion of an abiding gendered self. This formulation moves the conception of gender off the ground of a substantial model of identity to one that requires a conception of gender as a constituted social temporality. Significantly, if gender is instituted through acts which are internally discontinuous, then the appearance of substance is precisely that, a constructed identity, a performative accomplishment which the mundane social audience, including the actors themselves, come to believe and to perform.[35]

The theory that gender is created not by biology but discourse is best elucidated by Butler's own illustration of a baby being named:

> Consider the medical interpellation which (the sonogram notwithstanding) shifts an infant from an 'it' to a 'she' or a 'he,' and in that naming, the girl is 'girled,' brought into the domain of language and kinship through the interpellation of gender. But that 'girling' of the girl does not end there; on the

---

[34] Simone de Beauvoir, *The Second Sex* (New York: Bantam, 1952). p.249.
[35] Judith Butler, *Gender Trouble: Feminism and the Subversion of Identity* (London: Routledge, 1990). p.140-141.

contrary, that founding interpellation is reiterated by various authorities and throughout various intervals of time to reinforce or contest this naturalised effect. The naming is at once the setting of a boundary, and also the repeated inculcation of a norm.[36]

One may wish to respond to Butler by saying that she is articulating a half-truth. There is an important sense in which gendered identity is partly formed through society and family giving us messages about what its expectations are. However, Butler shows no evidence of considering her insights to be only part of the truth. Quite to the contrary, she uses this partial truth as a building block for claims that go even further. Not only is gender identity not created by physical biology:

> That the gendered body is performative suggests that it has no ontological status apart from the various acts which constitute its reality... The body is not a being, but a variable boundary, a surface whose permeability is politically regulated, a signifying practice within a cultural field of gender hierarchy and compulsory heterosexuality.[37]

Salih sums up Butler's views:

> Gender does not happen once and for all when we are born, but is a sequence of repeated acts that harden into the appearance of something that's been there all along.[38]

With specific reference to Butler's illustration of baby-naming:

> A girl is not born a girl, but she is 'girled' to use Butler's coinage, at or before birth on the basis of whether she possesses a penis or a vagina. This is an arbitrary distinction, and Butler will argue that sexed body parts are invested with significance, so it would follow that infants could just as well

---

[36] Butler, *Bodies That Matter: On the Discursive Limits of Sex.* p.7-8.
[37] Butler, *Gender Trouble: Feminism and the Subversion of Identity.* p.136, 139.
[38] Salih, *Judith Butler.* p.66.

be differentiated from each other on the basis of other parts – the size of their ear lobes, the colour of their eyes, the flexibility of their tongues. Far from being neutral, the perception and description of the body (It's a girl, etc.) is an interpellative performative statement, and the language that seems merely to describe the body actually constitutes it. Butler is not refuting the existence of matter, but she insists that matter can have no status outside a discourse that is always constitutive, always interpellative, always performative.[39]

Clearly, Butler's vision of freedom from gender is a radical form of freedom. However, as has been demonstrated, she is far from a lone voice making these arguments. Butler did receive criticism for her arguments in *Gender Trouble*. Some were concerned that her thesis denied the reality of physical bodies. For example, Barbara Epstein, founder of the *New York Review of Books*, wrote:

> The assertion that sexual difference is socially constructed strains belief... the vast majority of humans are born male or female.[40]

Butler attempted to deal with criticism that her theory denies the existence of physical bodies, by refining her views in *Bodies that Matter*.

> It is necessary to state quite plainly that the options for theory are not exhausted by presuming materiality, on the one hand, and negating materiality, on the other. It is my purpose to do precisely neither of these. To call a presupposition into question is not the same as doing away with it; rather, it is to free it from its metaphysical lodgings in order to understand what political interests were secured in and by that metaphysical placing, and thereby to permit the term to

---

[39] Ibid. p.80.
[40] Barbara Epstein, "Why Post-Structuralism Is a Dead End for Progressive Thought," *Socialist Review* 25, no. 2 (1995). p.101.

occupy and to serve very different political aims.[41]

In order to be fair to Butler, we must remember that Queer theorists may make arguments in order to provoke or stimulate a subversive perspective. As she says, calling a presupposition into question is not the same thing as doing away with it. Nevertheless, even in her attempts to nuance her theory, Butler continues to suggest that gender is better understood as analogous to drag dressing than biology:

> To claim that all gender is like drag, or is drag, is to suggest that imitation is at the heart of the heterosexual project and its gender binarisms, that drag is not a secondary imitation that presupposes a prior and original gender, but that hegemonic heterosexuality is itself a constant and repeated effort to imitate its own idealizations.[42]

The limitations to freedom imposed upon gender are thought by Butler to be constraints of not biology, but imagination:

> Sexuality that is constructed is still constrained – 'Sexuality' cannot be summarily made or unmade, and it would be a mistake to associate 'constructivism' with 'the freedom of a subject to form her/his sexuality as s/he pleases.' [...] On the contrary, constructivism needs to take account of the domain of constraints without which a living and desiring being cannot make its way. And every such being is constrained by not only what is difficult to imagine, but what remains radically unthinkable: in the domain of sexuality these constraints include the radical unthinkability of desiring otherwise, the absence of certain desires, the repetitive compulsion of others, the abiding repudiation of some sexual possibilities, panic, obsession pull, and the nexus of sexuality and pain.[43]

---

[41] Butler, *Bodies That Matter: On the Discursive Limits of Sex.* p.30.
[42] Ibid. p.125.
[43] Ibid. p.94.

Judith Butler's writings have given resolve and credibility to those who wish to free the world and church from what she calls 'heterosexist' repressive assumptions, which enslave people to the idea that our physical bodies play a significant role in forming our gendered identities.

It is understandable that the vast majority of recent writings on the topic of homosexuality have focused upon issues such as the Bible's teaching on the morality of homosexual acts. However, such writings are far from sufficient to make the intellectual case to those who reject them. For there are prior foundational concepts which form the context within which the better known arguments reside. Foremost among these foundational concepts is that of 'freedom.' It is vital that we explore this issue of freedom for at least two reasons: Firstly, if a person has been influenced to find a concept of freedom, analogous to that espoused by Butler, attractive, then he or she will be stoically unmoved by traditional Christian ethical arguments. They will be rejected out of hand due to being either incomprehensible or distasteful. Secondly, the church has been preoccupied with controversies about homosexuality. However this is merely the tip of the iceberg. What lies beneath is the real issue – freedom. It is inevitable that the foundational issue, the quest for a radical form of freedom, will (rapidly) take on new forms distinct from homosexuality. These may include questioning the limits and nature of transsexuality, recreational cosmetic surgery, paedophilia, sado-masochism and prostitution. All of these have been written about by Queer theorists – they have their arguments ready, and the culture is primed to receive them enthusiastically. Unless the church deals with the conceptual issue of freedom underlying the current debate of homosexuality, then we will be inadequate to speak to these other topics as they arise.

With all of that in mind, let us make a few observations about how Butler develops her vision of freedom.

4.   Freedom for all?

It has been demonstrated that Butler contends for a radical form of freedom which includes freedom from gender. What does her vision of freedom hold for those people who, like traditional Roman Catholics or Reformed Anglicans, believe homosexual desire to be a disordered love and homosexual acts to be culpable sin?

We suggested earlier that Queer theory treats all people as plastic – it changes and remoulds all of us. Butler's vision of humanity does this by setting up a new discourse of power, which favours homosexual desire and downgrades heterosexual identity. Freud was very interested in childhood development of sexual desires and identity:

> In view of the wide dissemination of tendencies to perversion we were driven to the conclusion that a disposition to perversions is an original and universal disposition of the human sexual instinct and that normal sexual behaviour is developed out of it as a result of organic changes and psychical inhibitions occurring in the course of maturation ... Among the forces restricting the direction taken by the sexual instinct we laid emphasis upon shame, disgust, pity and the structures of morality and authority erected by society.[44]

Freud's theory that early sexual desires were often perverted (to use his own language, which was not intended to be morally judgemental), developed into the theory of 'Melancholy' – the grieving for an imagined loss. Freud theorised that a little girl's sense of identity was formed initially by a sexual desire for her mother, which was repressed by society's condemnation of incest. The

---

[44] Sigmund Freud, *Three Essays on the Theory of Sexuality* (London: The Holgarth Press, 1962). p.97.

ongoing repression of this latent homosexual desire for the mother, would result in 'Melancholy'. That lifelong sense of grieving for a homosexual mother-love which was never realised, would actually become an important part of the adult woman's femininity. Thus, homosexual desire is actually the foundation of what is experienced as heterosexual desire.[45]

Judith Butler takes on and develops Freud's views, and argues that all heterosexual desire is melancholic, that is, predicated upon a latent, usually sub-conscious, homosexual desire. Butler admits that 'it may at first seem strange to think of gender as a kind of melancholy, or as one of melancholy's effects. But let us remember that Freud himself acknowledged that melancholy, the unfinished process of grieving, is central to the formation of the identifications that form the ego.'[46] She goes on to argue:

> Consider that gender is acquired at least in part through the repudiation of homosexual attachments; the girl becomes a girl through being subject to a prohibition which bars the mother as an object of desire ... homosexual desire thus panics gender. Heterosexuality is cultivated through prohibitions, and these prohibitions take as one of their objects homosexual attachments.[47]

In this manner, Butler presents homosexuals as more free than heterosexuals – only the homosexual has come to self-conscious awareness of who he/she really is. Melancholic gender identity is unstable. Butler can refer to heterosexual melancholic gender as a 'syndrome.'[48]

---

[45] Sigmund Freud, "Mourning and Melancholia," in *The Pelican Freud Library* (London: Penguin, 1917). Sigmund Freud, "The Ego and the Id," in *The Pelican Freud Library, The Pelican Freud Library* (London: Penguin, 1923). In the former Freud viewed this Melancholic formation as a pathological mental illness, in the latter he posited it as part of all ego formation.
[46] Sarah Salih, ed., *The Judith Butler Reader* (Oxford: Blackwell, 2004). p.245.
[47] Ibid. p.248.
[48] Butler, *Gender Trouble: Feminism and the Subversion of Identity.* p.71.

An aside in *The Uses of Pleasure* reveals that Foucault also assumed homosexuality lies under heterosexuality:

> No one would be tempted to label as effeminate a man whose love for women leads him to immoderation on his part; that is, short of doing a whole job of decipherment that would uncover the 'latent homosexuality' that secretly inhabits his unstable and promiscuous relation to them.[49]

Butler's view of heterosexuality reminds one of the comic scenes in John Irving's novel, *The Cider House Rules*, where a board is attempting to force a medical doctor from his job. This proves difficult, till a new board member arrives:

> The new man on the board was a psychiatrist; he was rather new at psychiatry, which was itself rather new. His name was Gringrich; even with people he had just met, he had a way of assuming he understood what pressure they were under – he was quite sure that everyone was under some pressure. Even if he was correct (about the particular pressure you were under), and even if you agreed with him (that there was indeed was a certain pressure, and indeed you were under it), he had a way of assuming he knew other pressures that preyed upon you (which were always unseen by you).[50]

Gringrich becomes the key to levering Dr. Larch from his post. The tactic eventually turns out to be levelling the accusation that Dr. Larch is a 'non-practicing homosexual.' This plan, theoretically impossible to argue against, poses some practical problems:

> If Dr. Larch were a non-practicing homosexual, what could they ever catch him at? 'We could catch him at being a homosexual, just not practicing as such?' Dr. Gringrich asked cautiously. Dr. Gringrich, in all his years of psychiatric service had never been moved to apply the label of non-practising

[49] Michel Foucault, *The Use of Pleasure*, vol. 2, *The History of Sexuality* (Middlesex: Viking, 1984). p.85.
[50] John Irving, *The Cider House Rules* (Reading: Black Swan, 1986). p.332-333.

homosexual to anyone, although he had often heard of such a thing; usually, someone was complaining about someone else's peculiarity.[51]

Irving's parody is prescient. It captures the oppressive sensation that Butler's ideology creates in those who are heterosexual. She favours freedom for homosexuality, but frames her argument in such a way as to deny heterosexual identity real dignity. She is claiming to have a better, more accurate knowledge of what goes on inside a person, than anybody who says they are not homosexual. In Butler's world of genders formed by discourse, the homosexual discourse reigns. We see the cultural outworking of this in television shows where the gay man is thought to have some valuable insight into a topic, simply because he is gay. Homosexuality is not only given preferential treatment as a lifestyle; it is thought to flow from deeper, more accurate self-understanding than heterosexuality.

In the end, Butler's conception of freedom is an absolute freedom which forces itself upon people who may not want it, or may not realise they want it. As such it is a freedom which enslaves. Dependent as she is upon Foucault, her philosophy of freedom falls prey to the classic response to the claim that all discourse contains hidden power-plays; the one who goes around exposing latent power-plays is actually making the greatest one. Butler builds on half-truths, and plays with concepts in a way that aims to subvert what she sees as the heterosexist oppressive regime of modern society. As with much of post-structural and Queer writing, this is a technique which is very successful at questioning; we do need that. However, it is weak at providing answers. The vision for society Butler offers is precisely the kind of oppressive system which she so passionately speaks against. She has Queered freedom into a system of thought which equates to freedom for all who agree with her, but how will the dissenters be viewed?

---

[51] Ibid. p.565-566.

5.   Ontology and Freedom

Judith Butler herself admits that the views she promotes are counter-intuitive. It may seem natural to assume that gender is something rooted primarily in biology, rather than being a cultural linguistic construction. That being the case it is important to highlight the fact that Immanuel Kant (1704-1824) casts his philosophical shadow over our modern world. In a post-Kant world, it is surprisingly reasonable to believe that gender is a linguistic construct.

Prior to Kant philosophers sought continually to push back the boundaries of that which is known about the world. After Kant, what is known is merely the categories of our own thinking. The tendency of Kant's philosophy to separate knowledge from ontological realities, may be seen from this comment:

> Our knowledge springs from two main sources *in the mind*, first of which is the faculty or power of receiving representations, the second is the power of cognisizing by means of these representations. Through the first an object is given to us; through the second, it is, in relation to the representation (which is a *mere determination of the mind*), thought.[52]

An often overlooked point is that both pre- and post-Kantian philosophy was human-centred; the difference was that while each pre-Kantian thinker put himself at the centre of *the world*, each post-Kantian thinker put himself at the centre of his or her *own world*. Before Kant, knowledge was assumed to lead to an appreciation of ontological realities. After Kant, with the mind hermetically sealed off from reality, the suggestion that something previously thought to be

---

[52] Immanuel Kant, "The Critique of Pure Reason," in *Kant's Critiques* (Radford: A & D Publishing, 2008). p.54.

ontological (like gender), was actually merely linguistic or a category of thought, began to make sense.

Few people have read the writings of Kant; nonetheless his philosophical views underpin much of modern culture's discourse. Not only does this background help explain Judith Butler's presentation of gender as performative linguistic discourse, it also explains why her writing (and that of other Queer theorists and the gay/lesbian movement generally) is so reluctant to make appeals to ontological realities.

That is, Butler represents a narrative in which traditional Christian gender ethics is portrayed as naïve and unintelligible because it bases itself upon some sort of appeal to an ontological reality e.g. A man ought not to seek to become a woman because he was born a physical man; or homosexual acts are immoral because God designed sex to function between a male and female. Both of the preceding statements are making an appeal to some sort of ontological reality, from which implications are then drawn. Such ontologically based claims are resisted by Queer writers such as Butler. They are presented as totalising, enslaving and heterosexist frameworks of thought.

Rather than appealing to ontology, Queer theorists prefer to utilise the rhetoric of autonomy, slavery and freedom. They identify their movement with other groups who have sought freedom from repression, such as women or slaves. Most gay/lesbian activists are so resistant to ontological claims, that even when one comes along which may be a support to their cause, they will feel uncomfortable with it and eventually reject it. The most notable example of this was the 'gay gene' theory. Many Queer writers now say that even were a 'gay gene' demonstrated, they would not want to use it as part of their defence of their lifestyle. It would limit their freedom too much, and conflict with a presentation of homosexuality as a free choice. Early denials of the significance of a gay gene may be found in the writings of discredited sex therapist, Alfred Kinsey:

> If all persons with any trace of homosexual history, or those who were predominantly homosexual, were eliminated from

the population today, there is no reason for believing that the incidence of the homosexual in the next generation would be materially reduced. The homosexual has been a significant part of human sexual activity since the dawn of history, primarily because it is an expression of capacities that are basic in the human animal.[53]

Some writers argue that since people can be found who have experienced sexual attraction to one gender, and then later developed attraction to the other gender, this is evidence that sexuality is not fixed by genes, but is flexible throughout life.[54]

The influence of Kant together with the remarkable political and cultural success of apparently non-ontologically based appeals to freedom, has made many Christians doubt the validity of their more ontologically grounded ethics system. Certainly, presenting ontologically based claims, to a person gripped by a system of thought which is influenced by Kant, will be ineffective. This is surely part of the reason that clear and frequent re-statement of traditional Christian teaching on gender related issues tends to not result in many people actually changing their views. Rather than giving up on our ontologically based ethics, or merely repeating our views ineffectually, we ought to expose the fact that writers such as Judith Butler are in fact themselves making ontologically based arguments.

As was demonstrated above, Butler uses Freudian theory to develop her theory that all gender sexuality is melancholic. Heterosexuality is actually built upon a repressed homosexual desire, which due to the nature of its repression, is inherently unstable. *This is an ontologically based claim.* Judith Butler is positing that at root, behind linguistically determined gender, there is an ontological reality which she can identify and write about. The ontological reality is repressed homosexual desire. The only distinguishing thing about

[53] Alfred Kinsey, Wardell P. Pomeroy, and Clyde E. Martin, *Sexual Behavior in the Human Male* (Bloomington: Indiana University Press, 1948). p.666.
[54] See for example, Simon LeVay and Elisabeth Nonas, *City of Friends: A Portrait of the Gay and Lesbian Community in America*, 1995, p.5.

the ontological reality upon which she bases her claims about gender, identity and sexuality, is that it is an ontological reality which is inherently unstable and in flux (due to it being repressed and often unacknowledged). This instability is what gives her a basis upon which to build a vision of gender itself being unstable, malleable and changeable.

The remarkable thing is that the argumentation made thereafter by Butler is identical in form to that put by traditional Christians. The only substantive difference is that the ontological reality she bases her argument upon is an unstable repressed homosexual desire, and the Christian bases their argument upon God's physical creation of a gendered person.

Thus Judith Butler's vision of gender is only as convincing as Freud's view of melancholic gender. In light of the impossibility of demonstrating Freud's theories of heterosexuality being built upon repressed homosexual desires, one wonders, did a writer such as Butler utilise Freud's arguments because deep down she wanted a basis – any basis – upon which she could build a gender identity that is unfixed and malleable? Did the desire for the freedom she sees in plasticity of gender drive her intellectual exploration from the outset?

Christians have no reason to fear using arguments which make appeals to a basis in ontology. Not only do Queer writers such as Judith Butler do so, the ontological realities appealed to by Christians are far more verifiable than Freud's theories. In a post-Kantian world, we would do well to point these things out to those who portray traditional Christian appeals to ontological realities as repressive or philosophically passé.

6.   Ethics and Freedom

Much has already been said to explicate the ethical views of Judith Butler, as they arise from her philosophical arguments for gender being linguistically and socially constructed. In her recent writings, Butler has herself applied her philosophy to specific social, political and ethical situations. She is consistent with her earlier writings when doing so; always having said that her works are necessarily political and ethical rather than merely theoretical. We will highlight some of the ethical applications that Butler has made of her philosophy.

As will have been noted from the extensive quotations we have drawn from Butler's work, her style of writing is dense, complex and not easy to follow. Colin Gunton observed that Karl Barth realised that the form a theology is presented in is intimately connected to its content.[55] Butler would agree. She writes in a manner which is difficult to follow because she wants to communicate by form, that her content is suggesting there is a difficulty to be experienced in appropriating her vision of reality. The form aims to unsettle and disorient because both content and form are Queer. An ethical vision of instability, change and uncertainty would not be well served by a style of writing analogous to the scholastic reformers. Butler's writings are full of questions, because she is seeking to subvert and question what appears as normal. The posture of asking questions and doubting norms has been posited by her as something which is of intrinsic ethical value:

> Virtue is most often understood either as an attribute or a practice of a subject, or indeed a quality that conditions and characterises a certain kind of action or practice. It belongs to

---

[55] Colin Gunton, *The Barth Lectures*, ed. P. H. Brazier (London: T&T Clark, 2007). p.145.

an ethics which is not fulfilled merely by following objectively formulated rules or laws... It is, more radically, a critical relation to those norms.[56]

Underlying the ethical valuing of asking questions and critiquing norms, lies the desire for a radical freedom. Freedom is a term Butler herself uses for the goals of her movement.[57] We have already questioned the extent to which Butler may be willing to extend freedom to those who hold views of gender and sex different to hers, and we have shown that her philosophy appears to have an inbuilt bias towards homosexuality. This is borne out by the manner in which she accuses another academic who defends the value of church and family in rehabiliting people suffering from confusion about their gender, of being 'intensely polemical.' She argues that his support of family and church in having a part to play in stabilising a boy's sense of masculinity, is actually proof that gender is socially constructed:

> The fate of masculinity absorbs his study because masculinity, a fragile and fallible construct, needs the social support of marriage and stable family life in order to find its right path. Masculinity needs to be propped up by various social supports, suggesting that masculinity is itself a function of these social organisations, and has no intrinsic meaning outside of them.[58]

Butler's utilisation of half-truths as part of a technique in theoretical enquiry may possess a limited value; we have defended this in our assessment. It is indeed a valid form of discourse. However when it is the dominant method, its value becomes more questionable. When it is used as a rhetorical technique against another person, as in the above quotation, it becomes unethical. It would appear that Butler's

[56] Judith Butler, *What Is Critique? An Essay on Foucault's Virtue* (2000 [cited 27.8.09); available from http://www.law.berkeley.edu/centers/kadish/what%20is%20critique%20J%20Butler.pdf. (accessed 27.8.09)
[57] Judith Butler, *Undoing Gender* (Abington: Routledge, 2004). p.21
[58] Ibid. p.90.

support of her version of radical freedom drives her to treat opponents who disagree with her in this manner, which she would object to strongly herself.

Her recent ethical writings show very clearly how her pursuit of this radical absolute form of freedom has the most practical ethical implications.

For example, she comments on the abortion debates, and so radicalises the nature of freedoms sought for the woman, that she assumes the woman who is denied the right to an abortion is herself being denied life:

> It seems important not to cede the term 'life' to a right-wing agenda, since it will turn out that there are within these debates questions about when human life begins and what constitutes life in its viability. The point is emphatically not to extend the 'right to life' to any and all people who want to make this claim on behalf of mute embryos, but rather to understand how the 'viability' of a woman's life depends upon an exercise of bodily autonomy.[59]

The freedom of a woman to have physical autonomy is so important to her that the possibility of life within the womb is a debate to not even be entered into.

Though her writings have done much to create the social conditions where approving civil partnerships and gay marriages are the touchstone of social acceptability, Butler (like many other Queer theorists and lesbian/gay activists) is so enamoured with her version of radical freedom, that she insists not only upon the right to gay marriage, but also the right to be free from that right:

> No doubt marriage and same-sex domestic partnerships should certainly be available as options, but to install either as a model for sexual legitimacy is precisely to constrain the

---

[59] Ibid. p.12.

sociality of the body.[60]

It is deeply ironic that a main plank in the popular arguments put for blessing of homosexual unions by churches, is the similarity between heterosexual and homosexual possibilities of commitment and faithfulness. The actual philosophical basis utilised by Queer writers to argue for the right to gay marriage is not the similarity to heterosexual marriage (that, as Butler points out is to subscribe to a prejudiced heterosexist presupposition). Rather, the basis for their case is a radical form of freedom and autonomy. This is the very thing that leads a Queer writer to argue for gay marriage in one publication, and freedom from gay marriage in another. It is a sad fact that in Western society marriage has been eroded and damaged by social pressures and changes in attitudes. Heterosexual marriage is a philosophical and social bond which is stable and has been eroded. Gay marriage is an unstable construct from the outset – judging from the writings of those most in favour of it. Churches which bless gay relationships will have to come to terms with the consequent relational instability which will in many cases follow in time. Queer theorists praise this as freedom; it is doubtful the reality will be as pleasant as they suppose.

Butler considers in detail the sad story of David Reimer. This person was born a boy with XY chromosomes. As a baby a relatively simple operation was botched and his penis was extensively burned, ensuring that it could not function normally. About a year later his shocked parents heard of John Money, at the John Hopkins University. He was a strong supporter of gender reassignment operations and the idea that gender is not determined by chromosomes. Money persuaded the parents to allow him to operate on the young boy, in order to fully remove his male genitals immediately, and to make plans for later creating a vagina. Money was particularly keen to perform this operation and monitor the child, as the child had a brother who could be monitored as a 'control' in evaluating the success of gender change. The boy David was renamed

---

[60] Ibid. p.26.

Brenda, and subjected to frequent psychological testing and physical examinations, aimed at exploring the child's sense of gender identity.

Money published numerous papers extolling the case as a successful gender reassignment project. However, despite the operations and being raised as a girl, between the ages of nine and eleven, David/Brenda began to urinate standing up – despite being bullied by other children for doing so. David/Brenda sought to play with trucks and toy guns and developed the deep seated sense of being a boy and not a girl. At the age of eleven the child refused to take oestrogen, and resisted considerable pressure to accept the full surgery which would construct a vagina. At this point a new set of doctors became involved, and the child began requesting and receiving male hormone shots, and had the earlier implanted female breasts, removed. A penis which partially functioned was constructed for David, as he by this point wished to be known, at the age of fifteen.

The case of David Reimer was used by academics and the media to defend both gender reallocation and the fixedness of gender. Butler believes that she has a way of viewing the situation which transcends both views. To her mind, the real problem with the David Reimer case is that society has norms of gender which it imposes upon people. We need freedom to not only move from one gender to another, but freedom from the very expectations currently associated with gender. So when David said that he did not feel he was a girl, the real problem was that cultural norms had been forced upon him to make him feel so:

> David understands that there is a norm, a norm of who he was supposed to be, and that he has fallen short of the norm. The implicit claim here is that the norm is femininity and he has failed to live up to that norm.[61]

In other words, the lesson Butler takes from David's story is that we ought to pursue a society which gives us a radical freedom from

---

[61] Ibid. p.69.

gender itself – not just freedom to swop genders.

Tragically, but perhaps unsurprisingly, David eventually committed suicide. This happened just as Judith Butler's book discussing this case was going to press. What is particularly interesting is that Butler does not conclude in her postscript about the suicide that this was a tragic case which bears out on several levels the impossibility of living out her philosophical visions of a gender which is always open to flux and change. Her desire for radical freedom remains an ethical absolute.

7.   Ministry and Freedom

There is much that Christian ministers can learn from engaging with Queer writers. We ought to be humbled by the scale of their achievements in the face of considerable opposition. Queer writers have persistently campaigned politically and sacrificially for the furtherance of their visions. Foucault modelled this. When speaking to a homosexual group he returned the 2,000 Francs payment saying, 'A gay man does not need payment to speak to other gays.'[62] The immense cultural impact of Queer theory is testimony to the practical and social changes that can be wrought by academic work. The insight of gay/lesbian activists in perceiving their need for intellectual underpinnings to their political ventures is one Christians would do well to learn from. We once had a similar tradition, which like Queer theory, saw all of life as a unified reality to be seen through a common lens.

Writers such as Judith Butler are eloquent witnesses to the fragility, brokenness and pain of living in a world which is not as it ought to be. In addition, many of the challenges she and others make against the totalising narrative of modernist ideals are necessary. Butler is one of those rare people willing to question and challenge even those things which may on the face of it have otherwise served her political interests. Would evangelical Christians be so enthusiastic to defend parts of Biblical teaching which might challenge aspects of our ministry, dear to our assumptions of growth and success?

Despite much to admire in Queer theory, the changes that it has effected in people create real challenges for ministry. The teenage boy considering homosexuality, the woman desiring cosmetic surgery, the sense of insecure gender identity that pervades much of

---

[62] David Macey, *Michel Foucault, Critical Lives* (London: Reaktion Books, 2004). p.125.

society and the difficulty of speaking up for Christian behaviour in public arenas of work, media and politics. How might Christians respond to a world in which we all appear to be plastic people?

It is helpful to remember that this is not the first time the Church has faced a situation where people embraced a fluid view of gender. It was a key tenet of ancient Gnosticism – that mystical blending of ideas from various backgrounds into an aspiration for secret knowledge and enlightenment. The *Gospel of Thomas*, quoted above, is not the only commendation of androgyny. Gnostics saw the separation of humanity into two genders as a necessary evil. So, in one retelling of the Genesis story, Eve says:

> Be quiet Adam!
> When there was no stability
> When there was no order
> We had but one form
> And we were both a single thing.[63]

The response of Irenaeus in the second century was to write his book *Against Heresies*. In this he outlined different parts of Gnostic belief in detail, and countered them by laying out the big picture plot-line of the Bible. He did this most famously by developing his doctrine of recapitulation. However he also paid attention to the plot-line of the Bible by giving detailed accounts of the ways in which it developed over time:

> The treasure hid in the Scriptures is Christ; He was pointed out by means of types and parables. Hence His human nature could not be understood, prior to the consummation of those things which had been predicted, that is, the advent of Christ. And therefore it was said to Daniel the prophet: 'Shut up the words, and seal the book even to the time of consummation, until many learn, and knowledge be completed. For at that time, when the dispersion shall be accomplished, they shall

---

[63] Werner Foerster, ed., *Gnosis: A Selection of Gnostic Texts* (Oxford: Clarendon Press, 1974). p.202-203.

know all these things.' Jeremiah also says, 'In the last days they shall understand these things.' For every prophecy, before its fulfilment, is to men full of enigmas and ambiguities. But when the time has arrived, and the prediction has come to pass, then the prophecies have a clear and certain exposition.[64]

Irenaeus was aware, more so than any of his predecessors, that the plot-line of the Bible has a cumulative weight of persuasiveness. All views of the universe which differ from the Bible are implicitly telling a different story – it just so happened that Gnostics were literally rewriting and editing versions of the Bible to fit their philosophies. A vital part of our response to Queer theory must be to take every opportunity to educate people in the plot-line of the Bible. This means not only giving people Bible overviews, but also helping them see how each part relates to the whole – and how the exercise of so understanding scripture actually has real life implications for issues such as gender, sexuality and identity. This cannot be done successfully if at the same time as teaching the plot-line of the bible, we are encouraging listeners to keep their beliefs private and separate from the society in which we live.

The obvious difficulty with encouraging ministers to teach the plot-line of the Bible, is that Queer thinkers, and a culture impacted by them and other post-Kantian views, have a deep suspicion of any meta-narratives. There is an instinctive suspicion of any story which claims an absolute authority over all people. How is this difficulty to be faced?

Queer writings actually contain the answer. As we have seen, Queer theory embraces and utilises all areas of culture to make its case; including biographical ruminations, films, novels, poetry and philosophy. As it does so it shows that it can reach and connect with all kinds of people, on various levels. The use of biography in

---

[64]   Irenaeus,   *Against   Heresies*   ([cited   27.8.09);   available   from http://www.newadvent.org/fathers/0103426.htm.

particular personalises the claims of Queer theory. When biographies are used by these writers, they are not simplified down to fit a preconceived narrative of what a gay or transsexual must be like – rather the detail of the actual life is explored and connections are made to other aspects of Queer thinking. There is a profound personalisation at work in Queer writings, which offsets the potential difficulty of communicating their meta-narrative.

Obviously, it would be wrong to set the personalising of Christian experience against the authoritative plot-line of the Bible. However, if we are to communicate the plot-line effectively to a generation suspicious of meta-narrative, we do need to highlight and give genuine space for the personal appropriations of this narrative. The reality of Christianity is appropriated in diverse personal ways.

All people have been changed by the impact of Queer theory – not just homosexuals. There are deep-seated fears and misunderstandings in both gay and straight people about what the claims of Jesus mean for their gender and sexuality. To counter this we would do well to let people hear, through testimonies and biographies, the personal stories of people living as disciples of the Jesus found in scripture.

In addition to giving meaningful attention to the plot-line and personalised appropriation of that plot-line, we would do well to highlight how the aspirations for freedom found in Queer writings, are met only in Christ and the Church. With this we shall conclude.

8.   Conclusion

We have seen how a desire for radical freedom underpins Queer theory, in particular as it is portrayed by one of its leading proponents, Judith Butler. We have exposed the ways in which her conception of freedom is unattainable, as it fails to give all people the freedom she covets unless they submit to her beliefs. We have also seen how her focusing on valid half-truths, such as the role culture plays in shaping gender identity, permits her to build a philosophical system that prejudicially favours homosexuality. The freedom so ardently sought by Judith Butler is simply not realisable in theory or practice, by the philosophical system she has shaped. The system collapses under its own weight; before one even considers the possibility that biology may play a larger role in gender and sexuality than Butler permits.

The Bible warns humanity about pursuing a radical freedom in which we overreach our status as creatures:

> **Psalm 2:1-6** Why do the nations rage and the peoples plot in vain?
>
> [2] The kings of the earth set themselves, and the rulers take counsel together, against the LORD and against his anointed, saying,
>
> [3] "Let us burst their bonds apart and cast away their cords from us."
>
> [4] He who sits in the heavens laughs; the Lord holds them in derision.
>
> [5] Then he will speak to them in his wrath, and terrify them in his fury, saying,
>
> [6] "As for me, I have set my King on Zion, my holy hill."

God's response to our pursuit of freedom apart from him is to establish the reign of his anointed king; Jesus Christ. The beautiful irony of this is that there has never been a more liberating and freedom-creating King than Jesus Christ. He is the one who said, 'If the Son sets you free, you will be free indeed.' (John. 8:36) All who come to him, willing to be changed by him, discover that their deepest longings for freedom are more than met by his grace.

Jesus, not sexual gender, is the lens through which the universe was designed to be viewed. Within the matrix of Christian theology, the freedom sought by Queer theory is experienced.

One of the distortions that results from looking at humans through the lens of Queer theory, is that the created givenness of bodies is swallowed up by an existential sense of damage – in extreme cases, the damage is an unfulfilled conviction that one was born with the wrong gender.

Orthodox, Biblical, creedal Christianity affirms that humanity bears both dignity and damage. Our exploration of Queer philosophy hopefully gives us more confidence in holding to the conviction that a great deal of the dignity humans possess resides in the created givenness of our gendered bodies. We have seen that the Queer Theorists' objections to orthodox Christianity are not so compelling as many assume. Few theologians have had a more personal, existential awareness of the radical power of sin, than Martin Luther. Nevertheless, he did not permit the damage done by sin to obscure the truth that God continues to preserve that which he has created:

> That whatever God creates, he also preserves is simply true and must be granted, but still it does not follow that human nature is unspoiled, which is corrupted daily.[65]

In other words, we must believe that humanity is damaged by sin – but not in such a way that we permit the preservation of God's creation to be undermined. This is but one application of a crucial rule of dogmatic theology – arising from the organic nature of

---

[65] *Disputation Concerning Justification*, Martin Luther, Works, Vol. 34. p. 176.

doctrine – no doctrine may be expounded in such a way that it swallow up another.

John Calvin highlighted the fact that all knowledge of self is interconnected with knowledge of God.[66] Karl Barth developed this insight polemically against secular quests to interpret mankind apart from Jesus. He dismissed such attempts at secular understanding as self-defeating, and applied Calvin's view:

> We certainly cannot consider man as a self-enclosed reality … We must understand him as open and related to God Himself. And we shall have to interpret this relation to God, not as something fortuitous, contingent and temporary, but as a necessary and constant determination of his being, so that from the very outset there can be no question of an understanding of man from which the idea of God is excluded. We can never acknowledge the genuinely godless man to be real man … This means that the knowledge of man as such includes and implies the knowledge of God; and again, that the knowledge of man is possible and attainable only from the standpoint of the knowledge of God.[67]

The above observations remind us that accepting gender as created, given and preserved by God, does not mean that one has to proclaim theologically simplistic interpretations of humanity. We seek to understand ourselves in light of our relationship to God, and in light of the shared human nature of brother Jesus bears (Hebrews 2:11). The pursuit of such self-understanding is a painful process, for all of us are damaged by virtue of living in the aftermath of Adam's sin. However, the journey of discovery ought not to be a lonely one, for the road to true knowledge is travelled by God's people together; the Church.

By the grace of God, we find in this present stage of our

---

[66] *Institutes*, John Calvin, I.I.I.
[67] Barth, Karl; Bromiley, Geoffrey William; Torrance, Thomas F.: *Church Dogmatics, Volume III: The Doctrine of Creation, Part 2*. Edinburgh: T & T Clark, 2004, S. 72.

journey that God reorders our lives and forgives our concupiscence. He does this for all his people, and he does it for each person through each other person. When we reach our homeland we will enjoy renewed bodies and the vision of God. Such theological realities resource true freedom – the freedom to rejoice in the dignity of our gendered, created bodies, and to help each other deal with the damage done to us by virtue of living in a sinful world.

Bibliography

Abelove, Barale, and Halperin, eds. *The Lesbian and Gay Studies Reader*. London: Routledge, 1993.

Alison, James. "The Gay Thing: Following the Still Small Voice." In *Queer Theology: Rethinking the Western Body*, edited by Gerard Loughlin, 50-62. Oxford: Blackwell, 2007.

Barth, Karl. *Church Dogmatics*, Volume III: The Doctrine of Creation, Part 2. Edinburgh: T & T Clark, 2004.

Beauvoir, Simone de. *The Second Sex*. New York: Bantam, 1952.

Berger, Peter. *The Heretical Imperative: Contemporary Possibilities of Religious Affirmation*. London: Collins, 1980.

Butler, Judith. *Bodies That Matter: On the Discursive Limits of Sex*. London: Routledge, 1993.

Butler, Judith. *Gender Trouble: Feminism and the Subversion of Identity*. London: Routledge, 1990.

Butler, Judith. "Imitation and Gender Insubordination." In *Inside/Out: Lesbian Theories, Gay Theories*, edited by Diana Fuss, 13-31. London: Routledge, 1991.

Butler, Judith. *Undoing Gender*. Abington: Routledge, 2004.

Butler, Judith. 2000. What Is Critique? An Essay on Foucault's Virtue. In, http://www.law.berkeley.edu/centers/kadish/what%20is%20critique%20J%20 Butler.pdf. (accessed 27.8.09.

Coffey, John. 1996. Life after the Death of God? Michel Foucault and Postmodern Atheism. In *The Cambridge Papers*, http://www.jubilee-centre.org/document.php?id=15. (accessed 27.8.09.

D'Emilio, John. "Capitalism and Gay Identity." In *The Lesbian and Gay Studies Reader*, edited by Abelove, Barale and Halperin, 467-76. London: Routledge, 1993.

Edelman, Lee. *Homographesis: Essays in Gay Literary and Cultural Theory*. London: Routledge, 1994.

Epstein, Barbara. "Why Post-Structuralism Is a Dead End for Progressive Thought." *Socialist Review* 25, no. 2 (1995): 83-119.

Foerster, Werner, ed. *Gnosis: A Selection of Gnostic Texts*. Oxford: Clarendon Press, 1974.

Fone, Bryne. *Homophobia*. New York: Metropolitan Books, 2000.

Foucault, Michel. *The Use of Pleasure*. Vol. 2, *The History of Sexuality*. Middlesex: Viking, 1984.

Foucault, Michel. *The Will to Knowledge*. Vol. 1, The History of Sexuality. London: Allen Lane, 1979.

Freud, Sigmund. "The Ego and the Id." In *The Pelican Freud Library*, 339-407. London: Penguin, 1923.

Freud, Sigmund. "Mourning and Melancholia." In *The Pelican Freud Library*, 245-68. London: Penguin, 1917.

Freud, Sigmund. *Three Essays on the Theory of Sexuality*. London: The Holgarth Press, 1962.

Gunton, Colin. *The Barth Lectures*. Edited by P. H. Brazier. London: T&T Clark, 2007.

Halperin, David M. "Is There a History of Sexuality?" In *The Lesbian and Gay Studies Reader*, edited by Abelove, Barale and Halperin, 416-31. London: Routledge, 1993.

Holmes, Mary. *Gender and Everyday Life*. London: Routledge, 2009.

Irenaeus. Against Heresies. In, http://www.newadvent.org/fathers/0103426.htm. (accessed 27.8.09.

Irving, John. *The Cider House Rules*. Reading: Black Swan, 1986.

Kant, Immanuel. "The Critique of Pure Reason." In *Kant's Critiques*, 4-383. Radford: A & D Publishing, 2008.

Kinsey, Alfred, Wardell P. Pomeroy, and Clyde E. Martin. *Sexual Behavior in the Human Male*. Bloomington: Indiana University Press, 1948.

Loughlin, Gerard, ed. *Queer Theology: Rethinking the Western Body*. Oxford: Blackwell, 2007.

Macey, David. *Michel Foucault, Critical Lives*. London: Reaktion Books, 2004.

Plummer, Ken. "Mapping the Sociological Gay: Past, Presents and Futures of a Sociology of Same Sex Relations." In *Lesbian and Gay Studies*, edited by Theo Sandfort, Judith Schuyf, Jan Willem Duyvendak and Jeffery Weeks, 46-60. London: Sage Publications, 2000.

Pustianaz, Marco. "Fashionably Queer: Lesbian and Gay Cultural Studies." In *Lesbian and Gay Studies*, edited by Theo Sandfort, Judith Schuyf, Jan Willem Duyvendak and Jeffery Weeks, 161-74. London: Sage Publications, 2000.

Pustianaz, Marco. "Gay Male Literary Studies." In *Lesbian and Gay Studies*, edited by Theo Sandfort, Judith Schuyf, Jan Willem Duyvendak and Jeffery Weeks, 146-53. London: Sage Publications, 2000.

Salih, Sarah. *Judith Butler, Routledge Critical Thinkers*. London: Routledge, 2002.

Salih, Sarah, ed. *The Judith Butler Reader*. Oxford: Blackwell, 2004.

Sedgwick, Eve Kosofsky. "Epistemology of the Closet." In *The Lesbian and Gay Studies Reader*, edited by Abelove, Barale and Halperin, 45-61. London: Routledge, 1993.

Smith, Barbara. "Homophobia: Why Bring It Up?" In *The Lesbian and Gay Studies Reader*, edited by Abelove, Barale and Halperin, 99-102. London: Routledge, 1993.

Stoker, Bram. *Dracula*. Ware: Wordsworth Classics, 1993.

Taylor, Charles. *A Secular Age*. Cambridge: Belknap Press, 2007.

Turner, William B. *A Genealogy of Queer Theory*. Philadelphia: Temple University Press, 2000.

Watney, Simon. "School's Out." In *Inside/Out: Lesbian Theories, Gay Theories*, edited by Diana Fuss, 387-401. London: Routledge, 1991.

West, David. *An Introduction to Continental Philosophy*. Cambridge: Polity Press, 1996.

Wittig, Monique. "One Is Not Born a Woman." In *The Lesbian and Gay Studies Reader*, edited by Abelove, Barale and Halperin, 103-09. London: Routledge, 1993.

LATIMER PUBLICATIONS